How to Be a Dragonfly

How to Be a Dragonfly

Patricia Debney

Smith/Doorstop Books

Published 2005 by
Smith/Doorstop Books
The Poetry Business
The Studio
Byram Arcade
Westgate
Huddersfield HD1 1ND

Copyright © Patricia Debney 2005
All Rights Reserved

ISBN 1-902382-71-4

Patricia Debney hereby asserts her moral right to be identified as the author of this book.

British Library Cataloguing-in-Publication Data. A catalogue record for this book is available from the British Library.

Designed and typeset at The Poetry Business
Printed by Antony Rowe, Chippenham

Cover image: 'Dragonfly Silhouette' (shot during the making of *Insect Flight Paths*) © Tim Knowles: www.timknowles.com

Author's photograph © Nancy Wilson

Distributed by Central Books Ltd., 99 Wallis Road, London E9 5LN

The Poetry Business gratefully acknowledges the help of Arts Council England, and Kirklees Culture and Leisure Services.

For Roderick

Acknowledgements

'August' was first published in *Sentence (a journal of prose poetics)* as '*', Spring 2005, Firewheel Editions, Texas.
'Pool Spider', 'How Not to be a Woodlouse' and 'How to Be a Dragonfly' were first published in *Connections*, Spring 2004, Arts Council England South.
'Out of This World' appeared as part of 'Jeep' in *Birdsuit 10*, Starwheel Press 2001.

With thanks to the writers and readers who supported me in putting together this collection, and in particular to Lynne Rees for reminding me, and Nikki Santilli for her critical understanding of the form.   PD

How to Be a Dragonfly won The Poetry Business Book & Pamphlet Competition 2004

PREFACE

Coming to prose poetry

We live in an age of porous frontiers – a condition that creates anxiety and opportunity. For most people, 'prose' and 'poetry' are mutually excluding opposites, so the phrase 'prose poem' is a puzzle. After a century of free verse, to accuse a poem of being 'chopped up prose' is still a ringing condemnation in the public mind… so what to say about poetry whose nature is not even to chop up its prose?

For a start, that it's no new invention. Baudelaire's petits poèmes en prose, an early landmark, pre-date free verse by half a century. Anthologies of French poetry will contain pieces in verse and prose layout, uncontentiously. Not so in Britain. For much of the twentieth century, the form seemed to have the flavour of aestheticism, preciosity, decadence. Oscar Wilde had dabbled in it, after all.

Even in North America, in a tradition always closer to speech than to song, where Whitman's long lines read like small paragraphs, prose poetry scarcely emerged. For most Modernists, vers libre seemed all the freedom they needed. Only in the later twentieth century, with different experiments in tone and register and form under way, did prose poems begin to appear alongside lined verse in the work of poets like (and as different as) Creeley, Ashbery and Simic.

The most recent revolution might be technological, more than literary. With its screen-sized single-takes, the internet has become natural home to a compressed form of short story, aka sudden fiction, flash fiction, short-shorts, microfiction. These pieces tend towards the wry, allusive, surreal, glancing and evocative – much like poetry. The outlets might be slightly different, but many writers contribute work to both. In our porous age, nobody's identity will be 'either/or', and it is no accident that a list of leading contemporary prose poets includes Margaret Atwood and Jayne Anne Phillips, women with reputations in the world of prose.

Patricia Debney's intelligent, artful pieces refer us to the ease and unselfconsciousness of prose, and a poem's exact feel for rhythm, for language, for the concentration created by that white space round the edges of the page.

Philip Gross

CONTENTS

Preface

i

13 How to Be a Dragonfly
14 How Not to Be a Woodlouse
15 Two Bugs
16 Pool Spider
17 Beaded Butterfly
18 Japanese Beetle
19 After Last Night's Rain
20 French Cicada

ii

23 Out of This World
24 Learning German
25 Crane
26 Wild Broom
27 For Eliot
28 Welsh Poppy
29 Orange-Man
30 Honeysuckle
31 Blue Moon

iii

35	What Happens
36	Venus in Transit
37	Titan
38	Occam's Razor
39	Prime Number 42
40	Bat and Ball
41	Blood-let
42	In the Arctic
43	August
44	Floating Poem
45	Lips
46	Red Fruit
47	Desire
48	The Place Where Fire Has Been

iv

51	Late Chrysanthemum
52	Grass
53	Pieris
54	Geranium
55	Azalea
56	Wild Orchid
57	Sunflower Sport
58	Wisteria
59	Clematis
60	Wild Garlic
61	Bluebell Wood

i

How to Be a Dragonfly

Never tuck in your wings. They grow out from your shoulders like two fingers, like hands. Learn to use them.

Let them, for instance, direct you in love: in the garden, under the apple tree in dappled shade; or above long brown grass, fast up the side of a hill. Or once, over a rocky valley, higher than you've ever been.

Or let them speak for you: a buzzing purr getting closer and closer. They know what you want to say.

Let them: plunge you into the water, let the egg slip out.

No one can see them moving. But they shine iridescent, keep you hovering just above the ground.

How Not to Be a Woodlouse

Avoid damp, dark places. Try not to hide. Your shell is for protection only.

Seek sunshine, dry weather, fresh flowers. Develop a taste for clean, clear water, and the smooth, pungent skin of just-picked fruit.

Celebrate the lightness of your touch, the way your feathery caress holds people still.

Remember that, like you, the world is not black and white, but made up of delicate shades of grey.

Two Bugs

Ants

When trapped, they strike out, releasing a quick sting. The skin there is hardly pink, but the burn spreads like pins and needles, only worse. Later in the day, the pain comes back, crawling beneath the surface, the place where it happened still unmarked.

Mosquito

If you bother something enough, it won't let you go. A week after it fades, one thoughtless scratch sets the bite off again, and the rest of the morning's an agony. It takes everything you've got to ignore the pleading when a touch, just to lay your hand there, would be so easy.

Pool Spider

One step too far and you're head over heels. At first it's refreshing, this surprise encounter. You've never liked nights alone and lately the heat makes something unsettled in you rise. All you did was get up and walk out into the cooler air, stretch, and close your eyes for a moment.

It's a funny kind of death. You feel your own insignificance. Everywhere you look is blue, blue water. You climb back up a step before you can move no further, then roll onto your back and curl your legs up over your body, await rescue.

Beaded Butterfly

I can't understand why you're blue. Not to mention ten times life size. Closer in, there's sky, dots of night, and a smattering of green and gold too.

I can't figure the tight roll of your pearly body, pencil-thin, or your copper antennae, blue bobbles at the ends, crossed once in permanent perplexity.

Or your lack of eyes. Your faceted head is blind, looks all directions. Your shiny wings are latticed open. The truth is, you'll never fly.

Even though the wrapped stem wired to your middle seems to angle you toward the sky.

Japanese Beetle

Some summers it hardly seemed worth getting up in the morning. Outside, the sun beat down, tarred-over potholes blistered. And on the roses, the beetles fed with the fury of the damned, their green metallic coats glittering.

The roses were your pride and joy, the only flowers the neighbours noticed. And for a short while, the petals were exquisite: the scented medium pink, the easily bruised white.

But every July he descended, crash-landed, over and over until you stopped counting. By the time he finished, your blooms were knotted and worn, bowed down, your green leaves stripped back to bone.

After Last Night's Rain

The children run out like pondskaters across the grass, zigzagging, their toes hardly touching. They spin, weave between what look like glossy button mushrooms sprung up overnight, a scene from *Fantasia*. They bring everything to life, leave trails in the settled dew like fairy dust.

Nothing lasts forever. By midday they are hot and tired, and we venture out, expecting casualties, expecting the creamy pieces littering the lawn. In the shade of a tree we come upon one: not a mushroom, plump chunks still good to eat – but a snail, its white splintered shell still wet with juices, disconnected, its body turned as though kicked, aside. And all around it, like spokes in a wheel, the others gather, stretching out their blind fingers in curiosity or sympathy.

French Cicada

One night we are sure you are moving around our sitting room, your single cry more and more urgent as you realise your predicament. But by daylight you are silent, feared dead. Even your compatriots outside are quiet, as if in mourning.

We search for your body, anticipating bug rigor mortis, feet stuck to the wall in eternal self-preservation. Come upon something high on the ceiling, green, long as a Gauloise. But it leaps away, over our heads back deep into the house.

Then, in the heat of the day, there's a racket from outside. Under the tree we find what must be you: bark-coloured, flat and inconspicuous, your sonorous wings folded round you like a shroud. We know what you look like now, too late.

We imagine your last hours, the song we thought we knew, the life we didn't. Keening from the branches explodes, stills everything to a point.

ii

Out of This World

Inside, you tick away, my watch with the diamond face. You are, without prodding, without cajoling or good luck, ready for the off, the race.

The first pictures look beamed back from another planet or the moon: empty eye sockets, flat expressionless mouth. Outline of a skin too thin to hold anything together. Your ribs curve up like a meal picked over, tiny fossil of Pompeii.

But somehow you are alive. They tell me this. I tell myself the same thing, adding that you are not a disaster waiting to happen, or part of the familiar emptiness. I sigh, and the ripples move across the screen an earthquake, a bomb, rough seas.

Learning German

In the early hours of the morning, I get up and go downstairs; someone's calling me, voice loud as blood in my ears.

I can't make it out, this conversation. Each night it locates a frequency, broadcasts somehow through my lungs, my bones, the ligaments in my legs. Impossible to ignore.

In the kitchen, I stand and listen. *What will she do next?* I wait, and as ever, it comes: I lift my hand, put the kettle on, a hot drink. *That is correct.*

Later, I retire to the sofa and television. There's a German soap opera on, trying to teach me the language. I watch the whole thing, knowing I can hardly understand a word, believing anything is possible.

Crane

You whine for your breakfast, the curious open-mouthed wail of someone disconnected, someone needing feeding. Each morning I hear you, glance up to see your slow motion filigree dance, your single wire leading down, like a beak dipping into water.

Wild Broom

– for my children

Twice now I've passed between the two of you on this path, growing tall and elegant at arm's length. Spurned lovers, I think. Or guards, your tough forest green evidence of military bearing.

Or siblings, perhaps. The same, but different, from the start. I stop to intertwine the softest shoots: now when you come into deep red and yellow bloom, you may grow together, or spring apart.

For Eliot

You knock me off my feet, like the Great Dane we once saw in a restaurant, who leaned so gradually, so pleasantly, into me that I didn't know I was tipping until I was on the floor.

How can I get my arms around you? You're a puppy who doesn't stand still, who I'll never hold all of again, arms and legs everywhere, wide hands out in front like plates, a dish to be filled, questions I can't answer.

You break me, make me whole again.

Welsh Poppy

– for Molly

Here you are, rushing in again at the last minute, settling where you will. From a distance I could confuse you with the others lining the road in bright yellow spring. But of course you are a delicate flower, no staid daffodil or trenchant dandelion. I can see as I get closer that you will always be young, your hat always blowing, half-covering your face now caught in laughter, your hand half up to hold it on.

Orange-Man

You've taken the old clementine on my desk, turned it sideways so the stem end's the nose on the wheel of a face. Drawn two eyes, the happy curve of mouth along the bottom edge. Then, seeing as it's soft, picked through the peel on top, teasing the watery flesh out into hair.

You thought we'd be angry. Instead, we put him in the freezer to harden up, and in time you remember: you bring him to lunch, set him on the table, all ice stubble and white shock up top, the spit of the old man you say you had in mind.

But after you've had enough, we fall silent. Decay sets in. Black spots appear, puckers and pits. He sags, bags onto the table-top. And his bright red smile wobbles, like a cry or laughter just beginning.

When you're asleep, we slip him in the bin.

Honeysuckle

Your mother, always in the sun, has died and come back to life who knows how many times, her frugal sweet smelling blooms a constant echo of fuller days.

And you. How did you get all the way over there, no support in deep shade? You're trailing along the ground now, still growing, soft stems pliable with moisture, leaves purplish and easily bruised.

You need transplanting, best in partial shade; you need something to hang onto. How does this look, this leafless tree? Wind your arms through its dying branches, give it new life. In this part of the garden you can let your flowers bloom just out of sight.

Blue Moon

You show me what got you started, someone's computer image of the impossible: the familiar white plate suspended in a deep twilight sky; the black silhouettes of ordinary houses and pine trees pasted across the bottom edge.

Not *once upon a time*. Yet, somehow, it's the beginning of your story: the one where a little boy, not unlike you, journeys into the night alone, solves puzzles to gather gold coins. He is becoming magical, you tell me. Later, he will ride on air.

iii

What Happens

Like an organ warming up, it starts with a long, low note, only from here it's not even like the rumble of a passing plane, or traffic in the distance. Not even like white noise, when we stop listening.

We can't hear it, so who is to know that it will go on? Who knows how it feels to be trapped, to be pressed up against a wall, unable to breathe. To want to fly.

The long low notes become a lament, the compression of air more and more frequent, building like a house, like a church pointing heavenward, a fugue of sound that rises.

Until at last it bursts into song. The mountain dissolves. Of course we throw our hands up in disbelief, shield our faces from the ash.

Venus in Transit

Similar in density and size to the Earth, Venus is known as the 'inside out' planet

This is what we think we look like to someone else, a stealthy glance in a shop window, our profile in passing, as close as we get to a mirror in motion. We see ourselves in its place, our place in the universe.

It wears its heart on its sleeve, all volcanic fury, sulphur and grief – but here it could just as well be a fly juddering on a camera lens, or a speck of paint that changes in the changing light. There's no hope to know the full extent of our own boiling, our rumblings deep inside. Across the blank face of the sun, white as an open eye, the flat black disc passes. No place for the depths we might sink to, the metal so hot we can only think, when we get there, of ice.

Titan

Saturn's largest moon

It's common knowledge you're a chip off the old block: look how your atmosphere curls like hers, a child who keeps some things hidden.

So it's only a matter of time before the pointing finger breaks through, rubs a spot on your surface sore. Before there's a mosquito hum in your ear, and then the tape-recorded message: *I know you better than you know yourself.*

Like it or not, you resemble her. And now the light strikes your clouds in a gasp of orange streaked red. Now she tells you what it's called, bringing with it a longing you never knew you had: *sunrise.*

Sunrise. You see it too. Now, like us, you are vulnerable. Now you can be hurt.

Occam's Razor

'No more things should be presumed to exist than are absolutely necessary.' – Mark Haddon

Is this to suggest shaving off the edge of something, the fine hairs we don't register, the nape of the neck? Or how a blade is good for separating one thing from another carefully, into lines of soil, salt or sand?

Or is it all about not nicking the skin? After all: *what you don't know can't hurt you*, and *if you can't beat 'em, join 'em*. Is it about not letting anything else in?

The thing about a blade is that it goes on cutting. You can't blame its instinct, the way it slices. The way, each day, it gets closer. Until only your life is necessary. And even that, eventually, will be thrown into question.

Prime Number 42

We need to know you're for real, not just some illusion, but bona fide *one of a kind*.

After all, almost everything is made up of components, the pieces of our lives: foundation, construction, selling point. Everything has angles and fractions. So it makes sense that we look for *second thoughts*, for *other hands*, and even, *etc*. First we look for a way to hook you and reel you in.

On screen, your seven point eight million digits snake down in scales, a shimmering skin. We throw everything at you, all manner of dissection, but the surface holds – it's not that long before we have to believe what we've always known: that nothing can break you, or make you, for that matter. Your lowest common denominator is only ever you.

We get exactly what we came for, and throw the rest back in. Here, you can pretend: one swish of your tail, and you're gone.

Bat and Ball

She tosses it up herself, that's what's unusual about it, no pitcher. It's a softball, the red stitching like sutures, bird prints, semi-circled round it. She feels the weight of it in her palm, then there's the practised release, up past her head, the partial descent, seeming to hover in front of her for a moment.

Sometimes she's on proper dirt, the wide net redundant behind her. But mostly she's in a field, any field anywhere, and the sky is opaque. And she's got the worn wooden bat, weighted at the end, resting on her right shoulder, the loosening tapes held on by her right hand.

The ball spins up, and as she gets her eye in, she brings her left hand to the bat too, lifting it off her shoulder, poised now by her ear.

She never misses. That's what's unusual too. She arcs the ball clear out over the field every time; it would be a home run only she doesn't move. And as soon as she brings the bat back, there's another white leather ball in her hand. So she does it again.

Turns out it's not about hitting the ball. It's about the way it always disappears into thin air.

Blood-let

All we see is red, and that rarely, although there are white cells too of course, and the clear, indefinable stuff that makes a highway, a smooth passage for it all, plasma. Today it's happening in the car again, alone on an empty road. I glance over while driving, watch the leak of it, the thread-like trickle across the grey upholstery. Funny how it drips like *slow and steady wins the race*, only it's losing. It's losing so bad, people turn away. So bad I can strike a match, and nothing, but nothing, catches light. So I don't know how, through years of it, I'm able to survive.

In the Arctic

It's hard to open your eyes. The sun doesn't warm, but blinds, bleaches the thin layer of ice, lightens the heavy drift. In time you learn it holds your weight, and you venture out. Only: no one tells you your fur isn't white, but transparent, the strands thick as quills, and not soft. No one tells you that all you can do is reflect the glare of your surroundings. That you're really just part of the scenery.

August

Leaving the dusting and dishes, you go outside. Here, the pots need water, dead flowers beheading, stiffened sheets unpegging. And the plums all down the driveway writhe with flies and wasps, their frantic buzzing reaching you like music swelling. The sun bakes, turns everything to dust.

You want to wring your hands like you've seen your grandmother do many times. You want to see a child's neck bent over a buttercup, completely still. Or a bird take flight. You want something. Anything. Waiting for it like waiting for a storm. You feel like crying.

The wind never rises. The light blinds. And going in, the darkness takes time to clear.

Floating Poem

– for Suzanne

In the attic room, you lie on your back next to her, imagining the sky. You think of the stars, endless and multiplying, and the fringe of pine trees leaning in like telescopes, pointing the way.

She lies on her side, fingers splayed. She thinks of you, all your soft crevices. She imagines the curve of your chin in her hand, the curve of your breast, the expanding universe she will never know the end of.

Lips

– for Roderick

1. Not very significant, you might say. And I'd agree, except that I went to a shop today to try to find something to make them redder. And that I look for the colour of them all around me. And that orange doesn't work.

2. One reason: so you know where to kiss. The skin is funnelled, runnelled, so that like paper folded then unfolded, it creases along the lines into perfect position.

3. Or: superconductor. There's no resisting your electricity. Whatever you pass to me I carry, like a string vibrates forever in space, until the other end touches down, liquefies in the growing heat.

Red Fruit

Slice it through the right way and it's a flattened-out frog, all arms and legs. Suck the seeds away and it's a flower, a snowflake held up to the light. Bite one edge and it cuts through to skin. Test it, tease it with your tongue, then strip it all the way around.

Slide it in your mouth, finally melt it to flesh.

Desire

It's easy to pick up, one of thousands of motes flying around a room. The sunlight comes in, catches it all in cross beam so the air seems full of them, impossible to ignore, and suddenly we have to walk through it to get anywhere.

The first casualties come over in a fever – it's all in the eyes, or is it in the mouth, the hands, the flush. They are suffering; it's clear they need to lie down. Within minutes, the telegram has done the circuit: *heartsickness* stop *old flame* stop *brand new*. People turn to each other like dancers for the next dance, hand on hip, lick of the lips.

All day it seems the weeping willow, the beach blue sky, the faltering piano playing, have been in a sort of conversation. When it reaches her she turns, puts a hand out as if to steady, sees the back of your head, just leaving.

The Place Where Fire Has Been

It's a safe bet that somewhere in these woods we'll come upon it. Some people just know where to keep looking, the spot to go back to and dig. When we find it, if we find it, it might be an unassuming piece of something. Hard at first to imagine it might once have been next to another, that it might have felt the weight of live wood, the sweet pressure of heat building, the first flickering, then the spreading upwards, sinking down....

Easy to know we're changed. It razes, leaves us standing, facing the other direction: what we thought was north is south, and the other way round.

If we're lucky, it doesn't matter: somehow we align ourselves again, and the satisfying click of opposites happens nonetheless. Despite everything, the laws of magnetism complete us.

But sometimes a piece of something doesn't swing back. Sometimes it refuses to forget. And without an end to fix to, it agitates at first, then slows to longing. Sometimes the pine needles just fall and fall. So no one remembers anything anymore about where the fire has been.

Late Chrysanthemum

Just when everything else is dying, there's a last puff of colour rising above the brown: a deep red furred head, gold centred reminder of last summer.

The frost, everyone knows, is surely coming, maybe tomorrow, maybe by next week. The nights are colder. No one knows how long a single bloom can survive.

Like the prince we could throw our bell jar over it; we could travel the solar system to stop the sheep from eating it. But this morning, the first frost on the ground and the sun coming in sideways, the web on the gate lit by dew, I stop instead for what I thought I'd never know: a yellow ladybird, two magpies just outside the door. And my whole garden hung with jewels.

Grass

More grey than green up close, this network of fading blades near the ground. I want to comb it like my daughter's hair, pull the brown threads through; then run the palms of my hands over it, smooth it, guide the nap.

I could tease it out like that, slavishly untangle. Or I could hope for the best. It's as soft as a pillow even like this. And who would ever guess – in this light, the sheen is blinding, edible – that almost all of what we see is already dead?

Pieris

You used to shout to me across the valley, your bright salmon pink a streetlight in all the green, your waxy leaves bushing out as though freshly preened, a jewel in the crown.

And from up on the hill, I knew I could see further than you: past the laughably clean cows grazing on the hillock; and the picturesque oak angled from the wind through these parts in winter. All the way out to the rows of peaked mountains, like ripples of water from a stone thrown in, the centre somewhere else, and long ago.

Still, there must be something about the right soil. Miles away in my back garden, your new cousins have been nearly killed off by the frost. Today when I grasped their slight trunks and pulled, the roots came out easily and whole, like a last breath, still huddled in a ball.

Geranium

I've always known that it was possible. But in years of tending summer pots I've never known it happen: then today, like opening a door, I lift the foliage and find another stem stuck in, red wheel of colour already blooming.

Who put it there? Guilty children, tucking in what snapped off? The wind? I guess sometimes what's wrong can end up right. Put down roots. Mend the bit that broke.

Azalea

Some say you are already beautiful, your crisp oval leaves leaning toward the end of each branch, your points of pink gathered, bound up in cones.

And maybe you're at your best, bonsai-like by my front door.

But I'll take my chances. When it rains, I carry you kicking and screaming out from under the eaves, into fresh water and the wind.

Wild Orchid

Unknown soldier. I didn't know you were buried there, didn't know that's where you'd fallen, dropped all that long way down into hell.

It's true I was going to pull you up, hadn't studied your markings, your tiny trumpet blooms in one lilac cluster, so delicate as to be almost white. All I knew was that you appeared, suddenly, in a pot in my garden.

Perhaps *orchis militaris*. Even in winter there are vestiges that match: stiff straight stem, furry copper hat, slender, well-placed arms a little away from your sides.

But more likely *dactylorhiza fuchsii*: common spotted. I remember your leaves looked splashed with ink.

We may never know who or what you are. Or might have been. And as spring approaches, I wonder have I done enough, too much? You like undisturbed ground, apparently; you like to be left in peace.

Sunflower Sport

1. The first one's in the front row of a field, crowds of wide open faces pressing on it from behind, each turned just so toward the sun. Several smaller heads come off a skinny central stem, and it seems to wave, look all around, like the one in the family who's *not quite right*, peeking out from mother's heavy green leaf.

2. There's another soon after alone on the hillside, bending in the late summer winds, its wiry heads crouching over. I can see how it survives, adapts to any situation. Whereas another might catch the breeze like a plate, shear its brittle stem.

3. September now, unusually hot. All this is pure coincidence, has no meaning. Through the rising waves of a traffic jam they appear – bright yellow petals like fingers flexing, a dozen of them at least, among the rubble. They do not lean toward me, peer over the crumbling wall. Will not push the gate down if they have to.

Wisteria

Old as the front step, you don't have it in you any more, wizened beyond caring. Your feathered heads are pale as spent seeds, your twisted branches grey and nearly dead.

Only this morning, outside the window, the long thin blush of purple begins, deepens down the stem. I didn't know what you could do, how you could make me feel, with your rush of heavy, beaded blooms.

I'll let it happen, let you run riot over the wall. Then I'll cut you back, hard.

Clematis

You bob brightly through the fence this morning, wide purple head buffeted by passing cars, and look – over there's your cousin, splayed up against that house, lily-like, open-mouthed pink.

Today the sun is not shining. Will no one stop, even give a wave? You're the eternal optimists in this neighbourhood, you and your kind, full frontal to the road, never embarrassed: *take me, I'm yours.*

Wild Garlic

Ruff along the roadside, silky green collar. Here the spiky white blooms hold their palms up, brightening the undersides of bluebells. There, they light the path to your door.

Bluebell Wood

We long to catch it at its zenith, the moment when the purple mist seems most likely to rise up and swirl, whirl patterns around the trunks of trees.

We walk, hoping for a glimpse, a patch, of perfection. Meanwhile, the light comes in sideways, throws each stem longer, higher up. Shy heads of hung bells lengthen into the middle distance, skirts flattened as by a wind or smoothing hand. When we're not looking, they stand up, and begin to dance.

Patricia Debney was born in Texas in 1964 and grew up in Southwestern Virginia. As an undergraduate at Oberlin College, she wrote both poetry and prose but eventually specialised in the short story and in translation. After moving to Britain in 1988, she pursued an MA in Creative Writing at the University of East Anglia, and until recently concentrated mainly on the short story, with work appearing in a number of anthologies, including *New Writing*. In 2001 she won the Mathew Prichard Short Story Award and her stories have twice been shortlisted for the Asham Award.

With the birth of her second child she returned to prose poetry, a genre she had first explored in America. Her prose poems have since appeared in journals and anthologies, and in 2003 'Andamento' was a shortlisted winner of the *writers inc* competition. Her libretto for the chamber opera, *The Juniper Tree*, was premièred in Munich and London by Almeida Opera and the London Sinfonietta.

She is currently a lecturer at the University of Kent, and lives in Canterbury with her partner, a composer, and their two young children.